The
INDEPENDENT
Investigator

Tahirih Lemon

Published by Sacred Square Publishing Australia
sacredsquarepublishing.com
info@sacredsquarepublishing.com

First published 2005
This edition published 2019

© Text – Tahirih Lemon, 2005, 2019
© Illustrations – Andri Evaris, 2019

The moral right of the author has been asserted.

All rights reserved.
Without limiting the rights under copyright restricted above, no part of this publication may be reproduced, stored in or introduced into a retrieval system, or transmitted, in any form or by any means (electronic, mechanical, photocopying, recording or otherwise), without the prior written permission of the copyright owners and publisher of this book.

 A catalogue record for this book is available from the National Library of Australia

ISBN: 978 0 6485851 0 7 (pbk)

Cover design by Leisa Jones, Soigné Beauty & Design
Typeset by Helen Christie, Blue Wren Books
Illustrations by Andri Evaris
Printed in Australia

# The Independent Investigator

Dedication

This book is dedicated to Ashkan Akhtarkhavari, Carmel Akhtarkhavari, Pharan Akhtarkhavari, Nadim Bazyar, Alexander Green, Yavar Khalili, Elissa Lee, Roslyn Lee, Steven Lee and Connor McMaster.

Thank you for providing such interesting and insightful questions for this book.

Contents

Introduction	**1**
Chapter One	**3**
How do we know God exists?	5
If God is all loving, why does he allow so much suffering and wars?	6
How do we know that Baha'u'llah and Abdu'l-Baha are who they say they are?	7
How did the Bab, after being shot by 750 riflemen, disappear and then reappear alive in His prison cell?	9
How did humans first appear?	10
Chapter Two	**13**
How do we know we have a soul?	15
When you die, how do you know you'll continue to live in heaven, since you won't have a brain and you'll just be lying there?	16
What is our soul and where is it?	17
How do we know there is another world?	18
Where is the next world?	20
What is the next world like?	21
What do you do in the next world? Won't you get bored?	23
How do we know this is the real world or is the next world the real world?	24
How do we know we won't be reincarnated into an animal?	25
Why don't animals have souls?	27
Chapter Three	**29**
Is there a heaven or hell?	31
Does 'the Devil' actually exist?	32
Do angels really exist?	33
Why does the Bible say that Eve was created from Adam's rib, when this isn't biologically possible?	34
Was Jesus Christ really resurrected?	36

Chapter Four — 37

- Do your prayers actually come true? — 39
- Why do we need to do the obligatory prayer? It's just another prayer. — 40
- How many Houses of Worship do we have? Why don't we have more Houses of Worship around the world? — 41
- Do you need to go to a House of Worship to say prayers or can you say them anywhere and will they be as powerful and effective? — 43
- What does the symbol of the Greatest Name mean? — 44

Chapter Five — 45

- Does predestination exist? — 47
- Why is the number nine so special? — 48
- Can We Smoke? — 49
- Why can't we drink alcohol? — 50
- Is spending lots of money on lottery tickets gambling? — 52
- Do Aliens exist? — 53
- What does Baha'u'llah say about ghosts? — 54
- What do the Baha'i Writings say about psychic powers? — 55

Chapter Six — 57

- Why is education so important? — 59
- Why is it more important to send girls to school? — 61
- Why is marriage considered to be sacred? — 62
- Why can't women serve on the Universal House of Justice? — 64
- Will the Universal Language come before the Most Great Peace? — 65
- Will the poverty in third world countries ever stop? — 66

Chapter Seven — 69

- How do we know we will eventually have peace? — 71
- What is the Most Great Peace? — 73
- What is the World Order of Baha'u'llah? — 75
- Will we survive or will the planet blow up? — 77

Chapter Eight   **79**
   When we say we are Baha'i what does it mean?   81
   How can we practice our virtues? What is the best way
      to practice your virtues?   82
   Why don't we have more Baha'is around the World?   83
   Who was the first Baha'i in Australia?   85
   Who was the first Baha'i in America?   86
   Who can contribute to the Baha'i Fund?   87
   How much is enough to pay to the Baha'i fund?
      As a child can I contribute even a few dollars?   88
   How do you know when someone is ready to hear
      about the Baha'i Faith?   89

Glossary   **91**

Bibliography   **92**

Introduction

This book contains the answers to questions asked by young people just like yourself. The book is entitled *The Independent Investigator* because it is very important that you investigate spiritual truth for yourself. One of the principles of the Baha'i Faith is the independent investigation of truth.

It is important that you decide for yourself what is true and just. This is highlighted by the following words of Baha'u'llah, the Founder of the Baha'i Faith:

"O Son of Spirit!

The best beloved of all things in My sight is Justice; turn not away therefrom if thou desirest Me and neglect it not that I may confide in thee. By its aid thou shalt see with thine own eyes and not through the eyes of others, and shalt know of thine own knowledge and not through the knowledge of thy neighbour. Ponder this in thy heart; how it behooveth thee to be. Verily justice is My gift to thee and the sign of My loving-kindness. Set it then before thine eyes." (*Hidden Words in Arabic*, No. 2)

Keep investigating and continue to seek answers to your questions.

CHAPTER ONE

- The existence of God
- Human suffering
- Baha'u'llah and Abdu'l-Baha
- Miracles
- Evolution of man

How do we know God exists?

There are many signs of God's existence all around us; it's just a matter of looking a little closer. One explanation is that all things must have a creator greater than themselves. For example, a painting cannot paint itself. A book cannot write itself. A computer cannot program itself. Therefore, the very first people could not have created themselves; they must have had a creator.

Abdu'l-Baha said, "One of the proofs and demonstrations of the existence of God is the fact that man did not create himself … It is certain and indisputable that the creator of man is not like man because a powerless creature cannot create another being. The maker, the creator, has to possess all perfections in order that he may create." (*Some Answered Questions*, p. 5)

Another sign is that Messengers of God are sent to earth to teach us about the existence of a loving God, and how to live our lives. All of the Messengers of God suffered here on earth while bringing the teachings of love and unity and living their lives as an example to all of us. They sacrificed their lives for us. Would you suffer and sacrifice your life for something that wasn't true or that you didn't believe really existed?

If God is all loving, why does he allow so much suffering and wars?

It is not God who causes all these conflicts and wars to occur, but rather humanity itself. Abdu'l-Baha said, "… The material world is the world of corruption and death. It is the world of evil and darkness, of animalism and ferocity, bloodthirstiness, ambition and **avarice**, of self-worship, egotism and passion; it is the world of nature. Man must strip himself of all these imperfections …" (*The Promulgation of Universal Peace*, pp. 451–52)

One of the things that makes us humans unique amongst the rest of creation is our dual nature — that is, we have a lower nature and a higher nature. Our higher nature is our spiritual side and our lower nature is our material or animal side. Because of this dual nature we are able to choose how we act and behave. This ability to choose is referred to as our free will. Abdu'l-Baha explained that, "Some things are subject to the free will of man, such as justice, equity, tyranny and injustice, in other words, good and evil actions …" (*Some Answered Questions*, p. 248)

The following quote by Baha'u'llah highlights the fact that it is humanity who is causing so much suffering and wars:

> "God hath … decreed as lawful whatsoever He hath pleased to decree, and hath, through the power of His sovereign might, forbidden whatsoever He elected to forbid … Men, however, have wittingly broken His law. Is such a behaviour to be attributed to God, or to their proper selves? Be fair in your judgement. Every good thing is of God, and every evil thing is from yourselves." (*Gleanings*, p. 149)

How do we know that Baha'u'llah and Abdu'l-Baha are who they say they are?

The best way to judge whether Baha'u'llah and Abdu'l-Baha are who they claim to be is to look at how they lived their lives and to study their writings and teachings. Baha'u'llah has written over one hundred volumes of Holy Writings, which provide guidance and answers relating to every aspect of our lives!

Baha'u'llah was born into a noble and wealthy family and, if He had desired, He could have obtained a high position as a minister of the Shah (The King). Instead Baha'u'llah devoted His time to helping the poor and the needy. Baha'u'llah spent forty years of His life in exile and imprisonment because of His claim to be the Messenger of God for today.

Baha'u'llah spent four months in the infamous Siyah-Chal prison (The Black Pit). Baha'u'llah provides the following description of what it was like in this prison:

> "We were consigned for four months to a place foul beyond comparison ... The dungeon was wrapped in thick darkness, and Our fellow-prisoners numbered nearly a hundred and fifty souls: thieves, assassins and highway-men. Though crowded, it had no other outlet than the passage by which We entered. No pen can depict that place, nor any tongue describe its loathsome smell. Most of these men had neither clothes nor bedding to lie on. God alone knoweth what befell Us in that most foul-smelling and gloomy place." (*Epistle to the Son of the Wolf*, pp. 20–21)

Abdu'l-Baha, like His father, spent forty years in exile and imprisonment within the confines of the walls of the prison city of Akka. Abdu'l-Baha wasn't freed and allowed to travel to where he wished until he was an old man.

How many people do you know who would spend forty years of their lives being ridiculed, tortured, have all their belongings taken and then exiled and imprisoned in order to become famous? Baha'u'llah and Abdu'l-Baha suffered in order that we may have a better world in which to live.

How did the Bab, after being shot by 750 riflemen, disappear and then reappear alive in His prison cell?

You must remember the Bab is a Manifestation of God, and therefore able to perform miracles. Abdu'l-Baha explains this by stating:

> "The Holy Manifestations are the sources of miracles and the originators of wonderful signs. For Them, any difficult and impracticable thing is possible and easy ... From all the Manifestations marvelous things have happened." (*Some Answered Questions*, p. 100)

You need to keep in mind that for the Manifestations miracles are not important and they do not wish us to focus on these events. Miracles are only proof for those who were present to see them with their own eyes. Therefore, using miracles to help illustrate the greatness and **authenticity** of a Manifestation of God may be useless and impossible to prove.

How did humans first appear?

Abdu'l-Baha explains that man did not always exist as we are today. Man gradually evolved and developed. He makes it very clear, however, that man was always an original species and not merely an animal that has evolved. Abdu'l-Baha has provided us with a number of writings on the evolution of man; a few of these are stated below:

> "In the world of existence man has traversed successive degrees until he has attained the human kingdom. In each degree of his progression he has developed capacity for advancement to the next station and condition. While in the kingdom of the mineral he was attaining the capacity for promotion into the degree of the vegetable. In the kingdom of the vegetable he underwent preparation for the world of the animal, and from thence he has come onward to the human degree, or kingdom. Throughout this journey of progression, he has ever and always been potentially man." (Abdu'l-Baha, *The Promulgation of Universal Peace*, p. 225)

> "... The fact that the animal having preceded man is not a proof of the evolution, change and alteration of the species, nor that man was raised from the animal world to the human world. For while the individual appearance of these different beings is certain, it is possible that man came into existence after the animal ..." (Abdu'l-Baha, *Some Answered Questions*, p. 192)

> "... As a man in the womb of the mother passes from form to form, from shape to shape, changes and develops, and is still the human species from the beginning of the embryonic period — in the same way man, from the beginning of his existence in the matrix of the world, is also a distinct

species — that is, man has gradually evolved from one form to another. Therefore, this change of appearance, this evolution of members, this development and growth, even though we admit the reality of growth and progress, does not prevent the species from being original." (Abdu'l-Baha, *Some Answered Questions*, pp. 193–94)

CHAPTER TWO

The soul and the next world

How do we know we have a soul?

With medical advances many people have been resuscitated after having a near death experience. Most of these people have had very similar experiences while they were clinically dead and then brought back to life. Several of these people stated that they were 'floating' near the ceiling watching the doctors and nurses trying to resuscitate a body, which they soon realised was their body!

One of the proofs of the existence of the soul is our dreams. How is it that without eyes and ears we see and hear clearly in our dreams and sometimes even travel, although we are lying in bed asleep? Have you ever had a **déjà vu** experience? Abdu'l-Baha commented, "How often it happens that it (the spirit) sees a dream in the world of sleep, and its signification becomes apparent two years afterward in corresponding events. In the same way, how many times it happens that a question which one cannot solve in the world of wakefulness is solved in the world of dreams." (*Some Answered Questions*, p. 227)

Abdu'l-Baha also stated that, "… No sign can come from a non-existing thing …" (*Some Answered Questions*, p. 225). If we did not have a soul, we would not have déjà vu experiences nor perfectly sane people whom, when resuscitated, make such claims — nobody wants to appear as if they have lost their minds!

In the end, whether you choose to believe that you have a soul or not is a question of faith. It seems ludicrous to think that this life comes to an abrupt end. What is the purpose and justice in this?

When you die, how do you know you'll continue to live in heaven, since you won't have a brain and you'll just be lying there?

We know we will continue to live for all eternity through all the worlds of God because we have a soul. To understand how we can continue to live even without a brain in the next world you need to understand the properties of the soul. In the future, when we have greater harmony of science and religion, the existence of the soul will be common knowledge and children will learn about it and its properties in school.

The soul has a number of powers, one of which is our mental ability. We are able to imagine, think, understand and remember because these are properties of our soul, not our brain. All of these mental powers radiate from our soul, like the sun's rays radiate from the sun. The rays are not attached to the sun but are emitted from the sun.

"Now regarding the question whether the faculties of the mind and the human soul are one and the same. These faculties are but the inherent properties of the soul, such as the power of imagination, of thought, of understanding; powers that are essential requisites of the reality of man, even as the solar ray is the inherent property of the sun." (Abdu'l-Baha, *Baha'i World Faith*, p. 346)

What is our soul and where is it?

Our soul is a spiritual **entity** and, therefore, words are not able to describe its true nature, nor are we able to truly understand what it is. Baha'u'llah says, "... the soul is a sign of God, a heavenly gem whose reality the most learned of men hath failed to grasp, and whose mystery no mind, however acute, can ever hope to unravel." (*Gleanings*, pp. 158–159)

One of the explanations given regarding the immortality of the soul is, "The soul is not a combination of elements, it is not composed of many atoms, it is of one indivisible substance and therefore eternal. It is entirely out of the order of the physical creation; it is immortal!" (Abdu'l-Baha, *Paris Talks*, p. 91)

Abdu'l-Baha also states that, "... If you examine the human body, you will not find a special spot or locality for the spirit, for it has never had a place; it is immaterial. It has a connection with the body like that of the sun with this mirror. The sun is not within the mirror, but it has a connection with the mirror." (*Some Answered Questions*, p. 242)

We are also told that our soul is not in our body and therefore things that affect our body do not affect our soul. "... The human spirit is in one condition. It neither becomes ill from the diseases of the body nor cured by its health; it does not become sick, nor weak, nor miserable, nor poor, nor light, nor small ..." (Abdu'l-Baha, *Some Answered Questions*, p. 229)

Our emotions, however, affect our soul; for example, "If we are caused joy or pain by a friend, if a love prove true or false, it is the soul that is affected. If our dear ones are far from us — it is the soul that grieves ..." (Abdu'l-Baha, *Paris Talks*, p. 65)

How do we know there is another world?

All the Messengers of the past and Baha'u'llah, the Messenger for today, have spoken about the afterlife. How lucky are we, to be living in this day? We have been provided with a wealth of knowledge regarding not only how to live happily in this life, but also about the next life. Baha'u'llah has stated, "Know thou of a truth that the worlds of God are countless in their number, and infinite in their range. None can reckon or comprehend them except God, the All-Knowing, the All-Wise." (*Gleanings*, pp. 151–52)

Abdu'l-Baha explains that our disbelief in the next world doesn't mean that there isn't an afterlife. "Those souls who are pure and unsullied, upon the dissolution of their elemental frames, hasten away to the world of God, and that world is within this world. The people of this world, however, are unaware of that world, and are even as the mineral and the vegetable that know nothing of the world of the animal and the world of man." (*Selections from the Writings of Abdu'l-Baha*, p. 195)

Abdu'l-Baha asks us two very logical questions regarding the whole point of creation. "Consider the aim of creation: is it possible that all is created to evolve and develop through countless ages with this small goal in view — a few years of a man's life on earth? Is it not unthinkable that this should be the final aim of existence? (Abdu'l-Baha, *Paris Talks*, p. 92)

Even though numerous writings have been provided on the afterlife, it is only a glimpse, because words cannot truly describe it, and if we knew what it was really like, we wouldn't want to remain in this physical world any longer.

"Baha'u'llah says that were we to have the proper vision to see the blessings of the other world we would not bear to endure one more hour of existence upon the earth. The reason why we are deprived of that vision is because otherwise no one would care to remain and the whole fabric of society will be destroyed." (Shoghi Effendi, *Lights of Guidance*, p. 208)

Where is the next world?

Abdu'l-Baha provides many statements regarding the next world which explain that it exists, but not as a place, and it is different from this earthly life, and yet there is no real separation. This sounds confusing I know. All I can suggest is to read and meditate on the quotes below and you will gain a better understanding.

> "... The world of the Kingdom is **sanctified** from everything that can be perceived by the eye or by the other senses — hearing, smell, taste or touch ... In the same way love has no place, but it is connected with the heart; so the Kingdom has no place, but is connected with man." (Abdu'l-Baha, *Some Answered Questions*, p. 242)

> "... The souls of the children of the Kingdom, after their separation from the body, ascend unto the realm of everlasting life. But if ye ask as to the place, know ye that the world of existence is a single world, although its stations are various and distinct." (*Writings and Utterances of Abdu'l- Baha*, p. 1258)

> "Those who have ascended have different attributes from those who are still on earth, yet there is no real separation." (Abdu'l-Baha, cited in *Life Death and Immortality*, 1994, p. 120)

That the world of existence is a single world and, therefore, there is no real separation can be demonstrated by the fact that rocks and plants exist on this earthly plane with animals and humans; yet the rocks and plants are not aware that we actually exist. That is, the rocks and plants do not have eyes or ears or even brains so they cannot see, hear or understand us. Therefore, souls that have moved on to the spiritual plane are aware of us, but we are not aware of or able to see them on this earthly plane.

What is the next world like?

We are not able to imagine or truly know what the next world will be like until we personally experience it. We can gather from the Holy Writings that it is a much better world than this physical world. Baha'u'llah and Abdu'l-Baha want us to concentrate on perfecting ourselves in this life. Remember our main purpose in life is to acquire and develop virtues during this lifetime while we have a free will. If we knew what the next world was like we would not want to remain in this world for another moment. Below are a handful of quotes from Baha'u'llah and Abdu'l-Baha which provide a glimpse of what the next world is like:

> "The world beyond is as different from this world as this world is different from that of the child while still in the womb of its mother." (Baha'u'llah, *Gleanings*, p. 157)

> "At first it is very difficult to welcome death, but after attaining its new condition the soul is grateful ... It has been freed from a world of sorrow, grief and trials to live in a world of unending bliss and joy ... The souls of those who have passed away from earth and completed their span of mortal pilgrimage ... have hastened to a world superior to this. They have soared away from these conditions of darkness and dim vision into the realm of light." (Abdu'l-Baha, *The Promulgation of Universal Peace*, pp. 47–48)

> "That divine world is manifestly a world of lights; therefore, man has need of illumination here. That is a world of love; the love of God is essential. It is a world of perfections; virtues, or perfections, must be acquired." (Abdu'l-Baha, *The Promulgation of Universal Peace*, p. 226)

"The mysteries of which man is heedless in this earthly world, those he will discover in the heavenly world, and there will he be informed of the secret of truth; how much more will he recognise or discover persons with whom he hath been associated. Undoubtedly, the holy souls who find a pure eye and are favoured with insight will, in the kingdom of lights, be acquainted with all mysteries, and will seek the bounty of witnessing the reality of every great soul. Even they will manifestly behold the Beauty of God in that world. Likewise, will they find all the friends of God, both those of the former and recent times, present in the heavenly assemblage."
(Abdu'l-Baha, *Baha'i World Faith*, p. 367)

What do you do in the next world? Won't you get bored?

The next world we are told is so much more glorious than this world; all the mysteries that we were unable to solve will be known and unanswered questions will be answered. We will join family and friends we had shared a love with and converse with people from all ages. When Abdu'l-Baha was asked regarding the attitude towards death, He replied, "How does one look forward to the goal of any journey? With hope and with expectation. It is even so with the end of this earthly journey. In the next world, man will find himself freed from many of the disabilities under which he now suffers. Those who have passed on through death have a sphere of their own. It is not removed from ours; their work, the work of the Kingdom, is ours; but it is sanctified from what we call 'time' and 'place'. Time with us is measured by the sun. When there is no more sunrise, and no more sunset, that kind of time does not exist for man." (cited in *Divine Art of Living*, pp. 37–38)

According to the quote above we will continue to work in the Kingdom of God. Also remember the worlds of God are infinite!

How do we know this is the real world or is the next world the real world?

We know the afterlife is the real world and that we are spiritual beings having a human experience. We are here in this physical world to prepare ourselves spiritually for the divine worlds of God where we progress for all of eternity.

Abdu'l-Baha said, "Know thou that the Kingdom (of God) is the real world, and this nether place is only its shadow stretching out. A shadow hath no life of its own; its existence is only a fantasy, and nothing more; it is but images reflected in water and seeming as pictures to the eye." (*Selections from the Writings of Abdu'l-Baha*, p. 178)

In reference to this world Baha'u'llah said, "The world is but a show, vain and empty, a mere nothing, bearing the semblance of reality. Set not your affections upon it. Break not the bond that uniteth you with your Creator and be not of those that have erred and strayed from His ways. Verily I say, the world is like the vapour in a desert, which the thirsty dreameth to be water and striveth after it with all his might, until when he cometh unto it, he findeth it to be mere illusion. (*Gleanings*, pp. 328–29)

A quote by Baha'u'llah that sums up the worth of this world is, "… the whole world, in the estimation of the people of Baha, is worth as much as the black in the eye of a dead ant." (*Epistle to the Son of the Wolf*, p. 124)

How do we know we won't be reincarnated into an animal?

The belief in reincarnation is believed to have been around since ancient times, even before the Egyptians. Ancient people lacked an understanding of the nature of the soul and therefore conceived of the idea of reincarnation. The belief in reincarnation has also come about because people are not aware of, or do not believe in, the existence of the divine worlds of God which we are told by Baha'u'llah are infinite. According to the teachings of the Baha'i Faith reincarnation does not exist and that: "No revelation from God has ever taught reincarnation; this is a man-made conception. The soul of man comes into being at conception." (*Lights of Guidance*, p. 537)

We do not need to be reincarnated back into this life to help develop ourselves further spiritually. It is in this life that we are provided with opportunities to develop ourselves spiritually and prepare us for the next world. Rather than return to this physical life we continue to grow spiritually through all the worlds of God. "... God, through His Mercy, can help us to evolve characteristics which we neglected to develop while we were on this earthly plane. It is not necessary for us to come back and be born into another body in order to advance spiritually and grow closer to God." *(Lights of Guidance*, p. 539)

Abdu'l-Baha also stated, "... This material world has not such value or such excellence that man, after having escaped from this cage, will desire a second time to fall into this snare ... The return of the soul after death is contrary to the natural movement, and opposed to the divine system. Therefore, by returning, it is absolutely impossible to obtain existence; it is as if man, after being freed from the womb, should return to it a second time." (Abdu'l-Baha, *Some Answered Questions*, p. 286)

Therefore, in response to your question, no, you will definitely not be reincarnated into an animal. You are you, and you will be you, for all eternity, through all the worlds of God!

Why don't animals have souls?

Animals do not have souls because that is how God created them. Obviously, we become attached to our pets and miss them terribly when they die. Death however is a fact of life. "The animal spirit is the power of all the senses, which is realised from the composition and mingling of elements; when this composition decomposes, the power also perishes and becomes **annihilated**." (Abdu-l-Baha, *Some Answered Questions*, p. 208)

Our intellectual powers are actually properties of our soul; which is why people are able to create, invent and think about abstract things like the purpose of life, love, the Creator and so forth. Abdu'l-Baha has said ... "As well as having the perfections of the mineral, of the vegetable and of the animal, he also possesses an especial excellence which the other beings are without — that is, the intellectual perfections. Therefore, man is the most noble of beings." (Abdu'l-Baha, *Some Answered Questions*, p. 235)

He also said, "Man — the true man — is soul, not body; although physically man belongs to the animal kingdom, yet his soul lifts him above the rest of creation." (Abdu'l-Baha, *Paris Talks*, p. 85)

Even though animals do not possess a soul they are still a creation of God and should be treated as such. Animals do in fact feel joy, contentment, pain and fear like humans and therefore should be treated with kindness at all times. "For in all physical respects, and where the animal spirit is concerned, the self-same feelings are shared by animal and man." (*Selections from the Writings of Abdu'l-Baha*, pp. 158–59)

CHAPTER THREE

Some Christian subjects

Is there a heaven or hell?

There isn't a place up in the clouds with golden gates and winged angels nor is there is a fiery place below controlled by 'the devil'. Heaven and hell are not actual places, but rather a state of the mind or a condition of our soul. Heaven and hell can also be experienced in this earthly life "… The paradise and hell of existence are found in all the worlds of God, whether in this world or in the spiritual heavenly worlds." (Abdu'l-Baha, *Some Answered Questions*, p. 223)

The feeling of being in heaven is experienced when we love God and follow His Will. Heaven is the state of being nearer to God. Hell is experienced when we do not develop a loving relationship with God or obey His Will. Baha'u'llah explains very clearly the true meaning of heaven and hell in the following quote:

> "Where is Paradise, and where is Hell? Say: the one is reunion with Me; the other thine own self …" (*Writings of Baha'u'llah*, p. 229)

Abdu'l-Baha explained the true meaning of heaven by stating: "The outer expression used for the Kingdom is heaven; but this is a comparison and similitude, not a reality or fact, for the Kingdom is not a material place; it is sanctified from time and place. It is a spiritual world, a divine world, and the centre of the Sovereignty of God; it is freed from body and that which is **corporeal,** and it is purified and sanctified from the imaginations of the human world …" (*Some Answered Questions*, p. 241)

Does 'the Devil' actually exist?

People believed in bad spirits or devils long before Christianity appeared. The images of devils and their powers changed throughout history. The ancient Greeks and Romans believed in several gods who constantly fought with one another. As Christianity spread to these countries, the Christians began to believe in two powers. These two powers were good versus evil or in other words God versus 'the Devil' or Satan.

Abdu'l-Baha has made it clear that God has only created good and that evil does not exist. Evil is merely the absence of goodness. 'The Devil' was used as a **metaphor** to prevent people from sinning. The Baha'i Writings state that all people have a dual nature — a higher nature and a lower nature. Our higher nature is our spiritual side which is developed by praying and practicing the virtues. Our lower nature, which is our animal side, becomes stronger when we lie, steal, tease, act with disrespect and so forth. Abdu'l-Baha explains, "… The evil spirit, Satan or whatever is interpreted as evil, refers to the lower nature in man … God has never created an evil spirit …" (Abdu'l-Baha: *Promulgation of Universal Peace*, pp. 294–295)

Do angels really exist?

Many of the world's religions mention the existence of angels. Did you know that the word 'angel' is an English translation of a Hebrew word which means 'messenger'? You often hear of the expression 'my guardian angel'; this is a belief that everyone has an angel that looks over them and helps them in times of need.

What is an angel? Baha'u'llah explains that anyone who follows the teachings of God can become an angel. Angels are servants of God who spend their lives helping humanity and following God's Will. "By 'angels' is meant those who, reinforced by the power of the spirit, have consumed, with the fire of the love of God, all human traits and limitations, and having clothed themselves with the attributes of the most exalted Beings ..." (Baha'u'llah, *Book of Certitude*, pp. 78–79)

Abdu'l-Baha in His Writings stated that, "The meaning of 'angels' is the confirmations of God and His **celestial** powers. Likewise, angels are blessed beings who have severed all ties with this nether world, have been released from the chains of self and the desires of the flesh, and anchored their hearts to the heavenly realms of the Lord". (*Selections from the Writings of Abdu'l-Baha*, p. 81)

Why does the Bible say that Eve was created from Adam's rib, when this isn't biologically possible?

Before we explore the answer to this question let's review the actual quote from The Bible. Genesis 2:21–23, "And the Lord God caused a deep sleep to fall upon Adam, and he slept: and he took one of his ribs, and closed up the flesh instead thereof; And the rib, which the Lord God had taken from man, made he a woman, and brought her unto the man. And Adam said, This is now bone of my bones, and flesh of my flesh: she shall be called Woman, because she was taken out of Man." (*Holy Bible:* King James Version)

Abdu'l-Baha's response to the literal interpretation of this story is that "If we take this story in its apparent meaning, according to the interpretation of the masses, it is indeed extraordinary. The intelligence cannot accept it, affirm it, or imagine it; for such arrangements, such details, such speeches and reproaches are far from being those of an intelligent man, how much less of the Divinity — that Divinity Who has organised this infinite universe in the most perfect form, and its innumerable inhabitants with absolute system, strength and perfection". (Abdu'l-Baha, *Some Answered Questions*, p. 123)

It is obvious from Abdu'l-Baha's response that this story is neither scientifically nor, as you put it, biologically possible. Abdu'l-Baha further explains that this story has symbolic meaning and contains divine mysteries and universal meanings. He also says that the verses of The Bible have several meanings.

One explanation Abdu'l-Baha gives for this particular story from The Bible is that, "Adam signifies the heavenly spirit of Adam, and Eve His human soul. For in some passages in the Holy Books where women are mentioned, they represent the soul of man". (Abdu'l-Baha, *Some Answered Questions*, p. 123)

This means that Adam, who represents all of humanity, was made in the image of God. That is, all people were created by God and therefore all are really spiritual beings. God has given everyone a soul, which is represented as Eve. Baha'u'llah states, "O Son of Being! With the hands of power I made thee and with the fingers of strength I created thee; and within thee have I placed the essence of My light ..." (*Hidden Words*, Arabic No. 12) The 'essence of My light' is our soul, which, as pointed out earlier, is represented as Eve in the story.

Was Jesus Christ really resurrected?

Three days after Jesus Christ's crucifixion on the cross it states in the Bible that He was resurrected. The word resurrected means to bring back from the dead. Obviously when someone has been dead for three days, their body isn't suddenly going to revive itself — this is not possible nor desirable.

You must remember that what is written in the Bible has spiritual and divine meanings and not necessarily material and everyday meanings. What the resurrection of Jesus Christ really means is that, for three days after Jesus Christ had ascended to the next world, His followers were very upset and troubled and in shock and therefore didn't do anything.

During those three days it was as if the Cause of Christ (later known as Christianity) had died with Christ's body. After these three days had passed, Jesus Christ's followers began to once again spread His teachings and their faith and belief in Jesus Christ grew stronger.

Abdu'l-Baha said, "... The Cause of Christ was like a lifeless body; and when after three days the disciples became assured and steadfast, and began to serve the Cause of Christ, and resolved to spread the divine teachings ... His religion found life; His teachings and His admonitions became evident and visible. In other words, the Cause of Christ was like a lifeless body until the life and the bounty of the Holy Spirit surrounded it." (*Some Answered Questions*, p. 104)

CHAPTER FOUR

Worshiping God:
- Answers to prayers
- Obligatory prayers
- Houses of Worship
- The Greatest Name

Do your prayers actually come true?

Abdu'l-Baha provides the following answer:

> "God will answer the prayer of every servant if that prayer is urgent. His mercy is vast, illimitable. He answers the prayers of all His servants ... It is natural that God will give to us when we ask Him. His mercy is all-encircling." (*The Promulgation of Universal Peace*, pp. 246–70)

Keep in mind that the answers to our prayers may not be the answers we had expected. The answer may even be 'No'! Abdu'l-Baha explains that if we ask for things that God does not believe are in our best interest then He will not even answer our prayers. If everyone were to pray, "'O God! Make me wealthy!' If this prayer were universally answered, human affairs would be at a standstill ... It is evident that it would not be well for us if all prayers were answered. The affairs of the world would be interfered with, energies crippled, and progress hindered. But whatever we ask for which is in accord with divine wisdom, God will answer. Assuredly!" (Abdu'l-Baha, *The Promulgation of Universal Peace*, p. 247)

Imagine if everyone prayed to God to make them wealthy. At first, it's a nice thought and everyone is happy, right? Wrong. Most people work because they need the money; if they were to instantly become wealthy, they would probably quit their jobs. There would be no teachers to educate the children, no nurses or doctors to look after the sick, no one to grow our food, make our clothes, no one to collect our garbage, no police to enforce the law and so forth.

Why do we need to do the obligatory prayer? It's just another prayer.

Baha'u'llah has provided Baha'is with three obligatory prayers to choose from: the short, the medium and the long. Obligatory means compulsory. At the age of 15 years all Baha'is are to recite one of the obligatory prayers daily.

The obligatory prayer is not merely another prayer. Shoghi Effendi states, "… The obligatory prayers are by their very nature of greater effectiveness and are endowed with a greater power than the non-obligatory ones …" (*The Compilation of Compilations*, p. 239)

Abdu'l-Baha has also written that obligatory prayers are "conducive to humility and submissiveness, to setting one's face toward God and expressing devotion to Him." (*The Compilation of Compilations*, p. 232)

> "Know thou that in every word and movement of the obligatory prayer there are allusions, mysteries and a wisdom that man is unable to comprehend, and letters and scrolls cannot contain." (*Tablets of Abdu'l-Baha*, Vol.1:85)

> "Baha'u'llah has reduced all ritual and form to an absolute minimum in His Faith. The few forms that there are — like those associated with the two longer obligatory daily prayers, are only symbols of the inner attitude. There is a wisdom in them, and a great blessing, but we cannot force ourselves to understand or feel these things, that is why He gave us also the very short and simple prayer, for those who did not feel the desire to perform the acts associated with the other two." (On behalf of Shoghi Effendi, *Lights of Guidance*, p. 465)

How many Houses of Worship do we have? Why don't we have more Houses of Worship around the world?

There are currently nine Houses of Worship around the world. Listed below are the locations of these Houses of Worship and when they were built:

    Wilmette, Illinois, United States of America – 1953
    Kampala, Uganda, Africa – 1961
    Langenhein, Germany, Europe – 1964
    Sydney, Australia – 1971
    Panama City, Panama, South America – 1972
    Western Samoa, The Pacific – 1984
    New Delhi, India, Asia – 1986
    Santiago, Chile – 2016
    Battambang, Cambodia – 2017

The very first House of Worship was built in Russia, in the city of Ishqabad. It was built in 1908; however, it was demolished in 1962 after being damaged by an earthquake.

Several sites have been set aside for future Houses of Worship. It is envisioned that one day every local Baha'i community will have its own House of Worship.

> "The House of Worship forms the central **edifice** of ... a complex which, as it unfolds in the future, will comprise in addition to the House of Worship a number of dependencies dedicated to social, humanitarian, educational, and scientific pursuits." (*Kitab-i-Aqdas*, n53) This means surrounding the future Houses of Worship will be a number of buildings such as orphanages, schools, hospitals, and so forth. "Shoghi Effendi envisages that the House of Worship and its dependencies

'shall afford relief to the suffering, sustenance to the poor, shelter to the wayfarer, solace to the bereaved, and education to the ignorant.' In the future, Baha'i Houses of Worship will be constructed in every town and village." (*Kitab-i-Aqdas*, n53)

Do you need to go to a House of Worship to say prayers or can you say them anywhere and will they be as powerful and effective?

You do not need to go to a House of Worship to say your prayers; you can say them anywhere as stated in the prayer, 'Blessed is the Spot', revealed by Baha'u'llah. This prayer states that anywhere where God is glorified and praised is blessed.

> "Blessed is the spot, and the house, and the place, and the city, and the heart, and the mountain, and the refuge, and the cave, and the valley, and the land, and the sea, and the island, and the meadow where mention of God hath been made, and His praise glorified." Baha'u'llah

The most acceptable prayer is not determined by where you say it, but rather how you say it. This is highlighted in the following quote:

> "The most acceptable prayer is the one offered with the utmost spirituality and radiance; its prolongation hath not been and is not beloved by God. The more detached and the purer the prayer, the more acceptable is it in the presence of God." (*Selections from The Writings of The Bab*, p. 78)

There are also practical reasons why prayers may be offered anywhere. For example, there are currently only nine Houses of Worship in the world and therefore most people live too far away from these Houses of Worship to visit them regularly. Remember we have to say our prayers daily. Also, some prayers like the obligatory prayers need to be said in private.

What does the symbol of the Greatest Name mean?

> "… The symbol of the Greatest Name represents an invocation which can be translated either as 'O Glory of Glories' or 'O Glory of the All-Glorious'. The word glory used in this connection is a translation of the Arabic term 'Baha', the name of Baha'u'llah." (*Lights of Guidance*, p. 271)

Abdu'l-Baha explained that, "The Greatest Name … is the name of comfort, protection, happiness, illumination, love and unity … The use of the Greatest Name and dependence upon it, cause the soul to strip itself of the husks of mortality and to step forth freed, reborn, a new creature …" (*Lights of Guidance*, p. 267)

Keeping this in mind it is therefore important to use and display the Greatest Name with the utmost respect. The Greatest Name may be hung on the wall and used for jewellery. It would not be appropriate however to use the Greatest Name on stickers, T-shirts, as a tattoo or items that are used for everyday living.

CHAPTER FIVE

Miscellaneous subjects:
- Predestination
- Number nine
- Smoking
- Alcohol
- Lottery tickets
- Aliens
- Ghosts
- Psychic powers

Does predestination exist?

Baha'u'llah explains that there are two kinds of laws governing fate and predestination. Some things in life are irrevocable, that is they cannot be changed or undone. Other occurrences in life are impending, meaning they are about to happen. Those things in life that are impending can be avoided through prayer.

Baha'u'llah states that, "... The decrees of the Sovereign Ordainer, as related to fate and predestination, are of two kinds. Both are to be obeyed and accepted. The one is irrevocable, the other is, as termed by men, impending. To the former all must unreservedly submit, in as much as it is fixed and settled. God, however, is able to alter or repeal it. As the harm that must result from such a change will be greater than if the decree had remained unaltered, all, therefore, should willingly **acquiesce** in what God hath willed and confidently abide by the same. The decree that is impending, however, is such that prayer and entreaty can succeed in averting it." (Baha'u'llah, *Gleanings*, p. 133)

The above quote also highlights the importance of accepting God's Will, rather than insisting on our own desires. Baha'u'llah makes it very clear that if God were to reverse someone's fate that was originally irrevocable, then the harm experienced will be even greater than had it remained according to God's original plans.

Why is the number nine so special?

Nine is the number of sides Baha'i Houses of Worship have and often the nine-pointed star is used on Baha'i signage and literature. There are a few reasons why Baha'is have an affinity for the number nine. The following explanations have been provided by The Guardian, Shoghi Effendi.

> "Concerning the number nine: the Baha'is reverence this for two reasons, first because it is considered by those who are interested in numbers as a sign of perfection. The second consideration which is the most important one is that it is the numerical value for the word 'Baha'. (B=2, h=5, a=1, and there is an accent at the end of the word which is also = 1; the 'a' after the 'B' is not written in Persian so it does not count.) (Shoghi Effendi, *Lights of Guidance*, p. 415)

> "First, regarding the significance of the number nine; its importance as a symbol used so often in various connections by the believers lies in three facts; first, it symbolizes the nine great world religions of which we have any definite historical knowledge, including the Babi and Baha'i Revelations; second, it represents the number of perfection, being the highest single number; third, it is the numerical value of the word 'Baha'." (Shoghi Effendi, *Lights of Guidance*, p. 415)

> "Nine is the highest digit, hence symbolizes comprehensiveness, **culmination**; also, the reason it is used in the Temple's form is because 9 has the exact numerical value of 'Baha' and Baha, is the name of the Revealer of our Faith, Baha'u'llah. The 9-pointed star is not a part of the Teachings of our Faith, but only used as an emblem representing '9' ... Strictly speaking the 5-pointed star is the symbol of our Faith, as used by the Bab and explained by Him." (Shoghi Effendi, *Lights of Guidance*, p. 416)

Can We Smoke?

Smoking is one of the unhealthiest things a person can do. Cigarettes contain nicotine which is an active ingredient used in bug sprays and pesticides. Tobacco companies may add any of over 600 or more additives to cigarettes. Some of these additives are things like acetone, which is used in nail polish remover, and ammonia, which is used in toilet disinfectants. Tobacco companies know how addictive smoking is once you start and take advantage of this by advertising. The more people that smoke, the more money they make. If someone starts it is so HARD to quit.

What do the Baha'i Writings have to say on the topic of smoking tobacco? Abdu'l-Baha wrote, "... I wish to say that, in the sight of God, the smoking of tobacco is a thing which is blamed and condemned, very unclean, and of which the result is by degrees injurious. Besides it is a cause of expense and of loss of time and it is a harmful habit ..." (Abdu'l-Baha, *Baha'i World Faith*, p. 335)

Want to hear more? Abdu'l-Baha also stressed that, "... Smoking tobacco ... is dirty, smelly, offensive – an evil habit, and one the harmfulness of which gradually becometh apparent to all." (*Selections from the Writings of Abdu'l-Baha*, p. 147)

If you already smoke and cannot give it up, keep in mind that when fasting you must abstain from smoking between the hours of sunrise and sunset. "In one of His Tablets, Abdu'l-Baha, after stating that fasting consists of abstinence from food and drink, further indicates that smoking is a form of 'drink'. In Arabic the verb 'drink' applies equally to smoking." (*Kitab-i-Aqdas*, n32)

Why can't we drink alcohol?

It is now common knowledge that alcohol has negative and detrimental effects on individuals, families and communities. Alcohol is the number one drug problem of youth today. Unfortunately, teenage drinking, binge drinking and alcoholic poisoning are on the increase and teenagers have sometimes died or put other's lives at risk whilst drink driving.

There are several quotes which state why Baha'is cannot drink alcohol, unless it has been prescribed by a doctor as medicine "… Intoxicating liquor, if prescribed by a physician for the patient and if its use is absolutely necessary, then it is permissible." (Abdu'l-Baha, *Lights of Guidance*, p. 350)

Abdu'l-Baha explains that the reason for forbidding alcoholic drinks is because "alcohol leadeth the mind astray and causeth the weakening of the body …" (*The Kitab-i-Aqdas*, n144)

In one of His Tablets Baha'u'llah states, "Beware lest ye exchange the Wine of God for your own wine, for it will stupefy your minds, and turn your faces away from the **Countenance** of God … Approach it not, for it hath been forbidden unto you by the behest of God, the Exalted, the Almighty." (*The Kitab-i-Aqdas*, n144)

Baha'u'llah also states that, "It is inadmissible that man, who hath been endowed with reason, should consume that which stealeth it away. Nay, rather it behoveth him to comport himself in a manner worthy of the human station, and not in accordance with the misdeeds of every heedless and wavering soul." (*The Kitab-i-Aqdas*, p. 62)

According to the Baha'i Writings alcohol has a negative effect on your mind and body and is strongly condemned. These negative effects have also been demonstrated scientifically. You have been given the gift of reason and intellect, why diminish its power and capacity by drinking alcohol. Alcohol destroys brain cells.

Not being able to drink alcohol as a Baha'is is a blessing in disguise. This is one good reason not to be pressured by your friends to experiment with alcohol. Your true friends will respect your wishes.

Is spending lots of money on lottery tickets gambling?

Many people want to become millionaires overnight, which is why so many people purchase lottery tickets. When you study probability in mathematics in school you will discover that the chances of winning the lottery are very slim indeed. The Universal House of Justice has written:

> "As far as individuals are concerned, we have carefully studied the Writings of Abdu'l-Baha and Shoghi Effendi on this point and it is apparent that such subsidiary matters are not recorded in the Holy Texts. The Universal House of Justice is not prepared to decide at this time whether the purchase of lottery tickets should be permitted or prohibited." (*Lights of Guidance*, p. 358)

Do Aliens exist?

The universe consists of billions of galaxies, each containing billions of stars. We live in the Milky Way galaxy, which is believed to have over 100,000,000,000 stars, one of which is the sun! Do you really think we would be the only creatures God created to live in such a vast space?

Baha'u'llah wrote, "... Verily I say, the creation of God embraceth worlds besides this world, and creatures apart from these creatures." (*Gleanings from the Writings of Baha'u'llah*, p. 152)

He also wrote, "Know thou that every fixed star hath its own planets, and every planet its own creatures, whose number no man can compute." (Baha'u'llah, *Gleanings*, p. 163)

Therefore, the answer to your question is; yes, it is possible that aliens exist.

What does Baha'u'llah say about ghosts?

There have been many stories and movies made about ghosts. Ghosts are the spirits of dead people who are believed to be trapped in this world or who travel between this physical world and the spiritual world. Ghosts are believed to take many forms which may resemble the physical likeness and character of the person before s/he died. Some ghosts are believed to be friendly, while others are believed to be evil and wreak havoc like poltergeists.

Abdu'l-Baha makes it very clear that no ghosts exist as we believe, and that once we die our souls ascend unto the next world. Abdu'l-Baha stated that, "There are no earth- bound souls. When the souls that are not good die they go entirely away from this earth and so cannot influence anyone. They are spiritually dead. Their thoughts can have influence only while they are alive on the earth ... But the good souls are given eternal life and sometimes God permits their thoughts to reach the earth to help the people." (*Lights of Guidance*, p. 206)

What do the Baha'i Writings say about psychic powers?

A person with psychic powers is someone who is able to do things with his/her mind or soul which are considered to be extraordinary. For example, maybe they can read your mind, see into the future or communicate with spirits in the next world. According to the Baha'i writings psychic powers do exist; however, we should not use them in this world because they could cause harm, and we do not really understand the consequences of experimenting with such **phenomena**. Abdu'l-Baha explained, "To tamper with psychic forces while in this world interferes with the condition of the soul in the world to come. These forces are real, but, normally, are not active on this plane." (cited in *Baha'u'llah and the New Era*, p. 193)

The Guardian, Shoghi Effendi, also stated that "… These psychic powers were not to be used in this world, and that, indeed, it was dangerous to cultivate them here. They should be left dormant, and not exploited, even when we do so with the sincere belief, we are helping others. We do not understand their nature and have no way of being sure of what is true and what is false in such matters." (*Lights of Guidance*, p. 514)

CHAPTER SIX

Some Teachings and Principles of the Baha'i Faith:
- Importance of education
- Girls' education a priority
- Marriage is sacred
- Universal Language
- Poverty

Why is education so important?

There are three types of education and all are necessary; however, obviously a spiritual education is of the utmost importance because we are really spiritual beings merely having a human experience. The three types of education are: "… material, human and spiritual. Material education is concerned with the progress and development of the body, through gaining its sustenance, its material comfort and ease … Human education signifies civilisation and progress … Divine education is that of the Kingdom of God: it consists in acquiring divine perfections, and this is true education …" (Abdu'l-Baha, *Some Answered Questions*, p. 8)

Education is important for so many reasons. Regarding a spiritual education Abdu'l-Baha says, "… If he (man) is deprived of this education he becomes the manifestation of satanic qualities, the sum of animal vices, and the source of all dark conditions." (*Lights of Guidance*, p. 211)

Abdu'l-Baha also pointed out that we need a spiritual education to help us develop and strengthen the virtues within ourselves. "… The merciful God, our Creator, has deposited within human realities certain latent and potential virtues. Through education and culture these virtues deposited by the loving God will become apparent in the human reality, even as the unfoldment of the tree from within the germinating seed." (*The Promulgation of Universal Peace*, pp. 90–91)

Without a 'human education' we would not learn how to read, write and think for ourselves. It is very important that everyone be able to read the sacred Writings and independently investigate truth for themselves. This type of education also enables children to learn many important skills which may help them to earn a living later in adulthood.

We all have special talents which education can help us develop. Some of these are shown in our schoolwork, some in our service to our community and some through our sportsmanship, musical or artistic ability. Baha'u'llah states, "Regard man as a mine rich in gems of inestimable value. Education can, alone, cause it to reveal its treasures, and enable mankind to benefit therefrom." (*Gleanings*, p. 260)

Why is it more important to send girls to school?

One of the principles of the Baha'i Faith is a universal education. All children whether they are rich, or poor should be given the opportunity to go to school. The reason there is such an emphasis on the importance of girls receiving an education is because they are the future mothers of the next generation and therefore the first teachers of all future children. This is clearly explained by Abdu'l-Baha in the following quotes:

> "... most important of all is the education of girl children, for these girls will one day be mothers, and the mother is the first teacher of the child. In whatever way she reareth the child, so will the child become, and the results of that first training will remain with the individual throughout his entire life, and it would be most difficult to alter them. And how can a mother, herself ignorant and untrained, educate her child? It is, therefore, clear that the education of girls is of far greater consequence than that of boys. This fact is extremely important, and the matter must be seen to with the greatest energy and dedication." (*Baha'i Education: A Compilation*,1977, p. 46)

> "For mothers are the first educators, the first mentors; and truly it is the mothers who determine the happiness, the future greatness, the courteous ways and learning and judgment, the understanding and the faith of their little ones." (*Selections of the Writings of Abdu'l-Baha*, p. 126)

> "If it is not possible, therefore, for a family to educate all the children, preference is to be accorded to daughters since, through educated mothers, the benefits of knowledge can be most effectively and rapidly diffused throughout society." (*Kitab-i-Aqdas*, n.76)

Why is marriage considered to be sacred?

According to the Baha'i teachings, marriage is sacred and considered to be a divine institution. While marriage is not compulsory, Baha'is are encouraged to marry.

To understand the importance of marriage as a divine institution you need to look at the purpose of our lives. We begin our life in this physical world to acquire virtues to help us progress in all the worlds of God, which are spiritual worlds. When we are young, our parents help educate us spiritually and help us to recognise and practice the virtues we have within ourselves. When we get married, we grow spiritually by helping our husband or wife to continue to develop and practice the virtues. That is why Baha'u'llah stresses the importance of the spiritual nature of marriage.

Another purpose of our life is to know and love God. The wedding vow that the bride and groom repeat is, 'We will all, verily, abide by the Will of God'. By studying, praying and meditating on the various Holy Writings revealed by the central figures of the Baha'i Faith — that is — The Bab, Baha'u'llah, Abdu'l-Baha we will discover God's Will.

Baha'u'llah states, "Enter ye into wedlock, that after you another may arise in your stead." (*Epistle to the Son of the Wolf*: 49) This is another vital aspect of marriage and without it, humanity would become extinct! "... The primary purpose of marriage is the procreation of children." (Universal House of Justice cited in *Lights of Guidance*, p. 350)

One purpose for the creation of humanity is to carry forward an ever advancing civilisation. An important aspect of an advanced civilisation would be an end to war. How can we have peace in the world if we cannot even achieve peace within the family? Marriage is one of the basic building blocks for establishing unity in the world. Abdu'l-Baha highlights this when he says:

"The happenings in the family are the happenings in the life of the nation. Would it add to the progress and advancement of a family if dissensions should arise among its members, all fighting, pillaging each other, jealous and revengeful of injury, seeking selfish advantage? Nay, this would be the cause of the **effacement** of progress and advancement." (*The Promulgation of Universal Peace*, p. 157)

Why can't women serve on the Universal House of Justice?

When the principle of the equality of men and women is explored, this question often arises. We do not know the reason for this decision at this time; however, Abdu'l-Baha makes it very clear that in the future the reason will become evident and will be as clear "… as the sun at high noon." (*Lights of Guidance*, p. 612)

The Guardian has written, "People must just accept the fact that women are not eligible to the International House of Justice. As the Master says the wisdom of this will be known in the future, we can only accept, believing it is right …" (Letter on behalf of Shoghi Effendi, *Lights of Guidance*, p. 613)

In a letter on its behalf the Universal House of Justice has stated: "Baha'is believe that to gain a fuller understanding of the reason women are excused from membership of the Universal House of Justice, we must await the evolution of society, and, we are confident that the wisdom of women's exclusion will become manifest as society develops and becomes more united." (cited in *Advancement of Women*, pp. 126–7)

Regarding the status of women, the Universal House of Justice has written that "… the ineligibility of women for membership of the Universal House of Justice does not constitute evidence of the superiority of men over women. It must also be borne in mind that women are not excluded from any other international institution of the Faith. They are found among the ranks of the Hands of the Cause. They serve as members of the International Teaching Centre and as Continental Counsellors …" (cited in *Advancement of Women*, pp. 130–31)

Will the Universal Language come before the Most Great Peace?

A universal auxiliary language is definitely needed to bring about unity and understanding between the diverse peoples of the world. Abdu'l-Baha has spoken about seven 'candles of unity' required to usher in the Most Great Peace, one of which is the 'unity of language'. The Most Great Peace will come about gradually as humanity matures spiritually.

In response to your question, it appears as if the principle of a universal language will come before the Most Great Peace. All of the principles of the Baha'i Faith are required to bring about the Most Great Peace. Shoghi Effendi has stated, "The Cause will not attain its aim and order in the great reign of peace unless its principles are put into practice." (cited in *Waging Peace*, p. 92)

The Universal House of Justice has stated: "A fundamental lack of communication between peoples seriously undermines efforts towards world peace. Adopting an international auxiliary language would go far to resolving this problem and necessitates the most urgent attention." (*The Promise of World Peace*, p. 15)

Abdu'l-Baha has stated: "One of the great steps towards universal peace would be the establishment of a universal language ... Until such a language is in use, the world will continue to feel the vast need of this means of intercourse. Difference of speech is one of the most fruitful causes of dislike and distrust that exists between nations, which are kept apart by their inability to understand each other's language more than by any other reason. If everyone could speak one language, how much easier would it be to serve humanity!" (*Paris Talks*, pp. 155–56)

Will the poverty in third world countries ever stop?

At the moment in the world there are many people who do not have enough food to eat, who do not have fresh water, a roof over their heads, or schools for children. In other parts of the world we see the opposite. In those places, people can own several houses and cars, waste food and have more money than they can spend. An important teaching of the Baha'i Faith is to get rid of these extremes of poverty and wealth. Baha'is believe that, in the future, many people will be more willing to share, and an economy based on spiritual principles rather than the greed of a few will evolve.

The Universal House of Justice recognises the distress and concern this situation has on Baha'is; but it is important to remain focused on the long-term goal which is to help bring about the Most Great Peace. When humanity recognises the unity of all people, then people will not let their 'brothers' and 'sisters' suffer as they do now. The Universal House of Justice states, "It is understandable that Baha'is who witness the miserable conditions under which so many human beings have to live, or who hear of a sudden disaster that has struck a certain area of the world, are moved to do something practical to ameliorate those conditions and to help their suffering fellow-mortals." (UHJ, 1963–1986: No. 151.2)

The Universal House of Justice further emphasises that "... we must not allow ourselves to forget the continuing, appalling burden of suffering under which millions of human beings are always groaning — a burden which they have borne for century upon century and which it is the mission of Baha'u'llah to lift at last. The principal cause of this suffering, which one can witness wherever one turns, is the corruption of human morals and the prevalence of prejudice, suspicion, hatred, untrustworthiness, selfishness and tyranny among men. It is not merely material well-being that people need. What they desperately need is to know who they are, to what purpose they exist, and how they should act towards one another; and, once they know the answers to these questions, they need to be helped to gradually apply these answers to everyday behaviour. It is to the solution of this basic problem of mankind that the greater part of all our energy and resources should be directed. There are mighty agencies in this world, governments, foundations, institutions of many kinds with tremendous financial resources which are working to improve the material lot of human beings. Anything we Baha'is could add to such resources in the way of special funds or contributions would be a negligible drop in the ocean. However, alone among men we have the divinely given remedy for the real ills of mankind; no one else is doing or can do this most important work, and if we divert our energy and our funds into fields in which others are already doing more than we can hope to do, we shall be delaying the diffusion of the Divine Message which is the most important task of all." (UHJ,1963–1986: No. 151.5)

CHAPTER SEVEN

Peace in the World:
- Peace is inevitable
- The Most Great Peace
- World Order of Baha'u'llah
- Survival of humanity

How do we know we will eventually have peace?

We know we will eventually have peace because Baha'u'llah assures us that the world will become united. Baha'u'llah's Mission is the unification of all of humanity. "... Whatever our shortcomings may be, and however formidable the forces of darkness which besiege us today, the unification of mankind as outlined and ensured by the World Order of Baha'u'llah will in the fullness of time be firmly and permanently established. This is Baha'u'llah's promise, and no power on earth can in the long run prevent or even retard its adequate realisation. The friends should, therefore, not lose hope, but fully conscious of their power and their role they should persevere in their mighty efforts for the extension and the consolidation of Baha'u'llah's universal dominion on earth." (Shoghi Effendi, *Lights of Guidance*, p. 130)

> "We are told by Shoghi Effendi that two great processes are at work in the world: the great Plan of God, tumultuous in its progress, working through mankind as a whole, tearing down barriers to world unity and forging humankind into a unified body in the fires of suffering and experience. This process will produce in God's due time, the Lesser Peace, the political unification of the world. Mankind at that time can be likened to a body that is unified but without life. The second process, the task of breathing life into this unified body — of creating true unity and spirituality culminating in the Most Great Peace — is that of the Baha'is, who are labouring consciously, with detailed instructions and continuing divine guidance, to erect the fabric of the Kingdom of God on earth ..." (*Messages from the Universal House of Justice*, 1963–1986, pp. 126–7)

> "World peace is not only possible but **inevitable**. It is the next stage in the evolution of this planet." (UHJ, *The Promise of World Peace*, p. 13)

It is important to remember Baha'u'llah's promise of world peace and not to become discouraged and lose hope in the face of all the conflict and wars occurring throughout the world today. Many young people today fear there will be a nuclear war resulting in the destruction of the planet. The planet will not be destroyed; however, humanity will continue to suffer until it matures and brings about the Lesser Peace, which is the unification of all countries on a political level, and eventually the Most Great Peace, which is the unification of humanity spiritually and socially.

What is the Most Great Peace?

The Most Great Peace will unfold as the World Order of Baha'u'llah emerges. The Most Great Peace will be the spiritual, social and political unity of humanity. Prior to the Most Great Peace will be the Lesser Peace which will be the forming of a world commonwealth bringing about a political unity of all nations and states. The Most Great Peace will come about as more and more people acknowledge Baha'u'llah and accept His teachings and principles as the standard for all of the world's peoples. Shoghi Effendi states the Most Great Peace can come only "consequent to the recognition of the character, and the acknowledgement of the claims, of the Faith of Baha'u'llah." (*The Promised Day is Come*, p. 128)

Speaking of the Most Great Peace, Shoghi Effendi said, "Then will a world civilisation be born, flourish, and perpetuate itself, a civilisation with a fullness of life such as the world has never seen nor can as yet conceive. Then will the Everlasting Covenant be fulfilled in its completeness. Then will the promise enshrined in all the Books of God be redeemed, and all the prophecies uttered by the Prophets of old come to pass, and the vision of seers and poets be realised. Then will the planet, **galvanized** through the universal belief of its dwellers in one God, and their allegiance to one common Revelation, mirror, within the limitations imposed upon it, the effulgent glories of the sovereignty of Baha'u'llah ..." (*The Promised Day is Come*, p. 128)

It is important to remember that the Most Great Peace will come about through the efforts of the Baha'is in spreading the teachings of Baha'u'llah and actively participating in the Baha'i community and its administration. "First, there will come the Lesser Peace, when the unity of nations will be achieved, then gradually the Most Great Peace — the spiritual as well as social and political unity of mankind, when the Baha'i World Commonwealth, operating in strict accordance with the laws and ordinances of the Most Holy Book of the Baha'i Revelation, will have been established through the efforts of the Baha'is." (Universal House of Justice, *Lights of Guidance*, p. 437)

What is the World Order of Baha'u'llah?

The World Order of Baha'u'llah is a very vast topic that whole books have been written about. In very simple terms the World Order of Baha'u'llah refers to the time when His principles and teachings will be implemented throughout the world as the standard for all of humanity. The Administrative Order of the Baha'i Faith, which encompasses National and Local Spiritual Assemblies, Auxiliary Board Members, Counsellors and so forth, is currently in a very embryonic stage and will mature over time. The Administrative Order is merely an instrument for the operation of the World Order of Baha'u'llah. The World Order of Baha'u'llah is a goal which we as Baha'is are striving to bring about by teaching the Cause.

When the World Order of Baha'u'llah is established all of the world's people, regardless of what race, nationality, religion or socioeconomic background, will become united. All of the current racial, national and religious conflicts and rivalries, hatred and prejudices will be replaced with understanding, acceptance and cooperation.

There will be a world commonwealth with representatives from all the world's nations which will ensure the peace and security of the entire world. Shoghi Effendi explains some of the duties of this world commonwealth in the following quote:

> "This commonwealth must, as far as we can visualise it, consist of a world legislature, whose members will, as the trustees of the whole of mankind, ultimately control the entire resources of all the component nations, and will enact such laws as shall be required to regulate the life, satisfy the needs and adjust the relationships of all races and peoples." (*The World Order of Baha'u'llah*, p. 203)

"A world executive, backed by an international Force, will carry out the decisions arrived at, and apply the laws enacted by, this world legislature, and will safeguard the organic unity of the whole commonwealth ..." (*World Order of Baha'u'llah*, pp. 203–204)

To help bring about the unity of the diverse nations and races of the world through increased understanding, the following will be adopted: "A world script, a world literature, a uniform and universal system of currency, of weights and measures ..." (*The World Order of Baha'u'llah*, p. 203)

The Most Great Peace will unfold as the Baha'i World Order emerges.

Will we survive or will the planet blow up?

This is a common fear among many young people today, which is understandable since they are continuously bombarded by the media regarding all the conflicts and wars occurring throughout the world. According to the news it appears as if the only news worth reporting is bad news which provides very little hope. It's important to remain positive and to remember that Baha'u'llah assures us that peace is inevitable and therefore the planet will not be blown up. All the conflict, confusion and intense suffering in the world is merely a transitional phase which will pass. "... All we know is that the Lesser and the Most Great Peace will come — their exact dates we do not know. The same is true as regards the possibility of a future war; we cannot state dogmatically it will or will not take place — all we know is that mankind must suffer and be punished sufficiently to make it turn to God." (Universal House of Justice, *Lights of Guidance*, p. 436)

> "... the Baha'i Faith aims to eliminate all war, including nuclear. The fundamental purpose of our Faith is unity and the establishment of peace. This goal, which is the longing of people throughout an increasingly insecure world, can only be achieved through the Teachings of Baha'u'llah. Since it is only the Baha'is who can give these Teachings to mankind, the friends must weigh carefully how they will spend their time and energy and guard against associating with activities which unduly distract them from their primary responsibility of sharing the Message of Baha'u'llah." (Letter on behalf of the Universal House of Justice, *Lights of Guidance*, p. 436)

CHAPTER EIGHT

What is a Baha'i, and related topics?
- Practicing virtues
- First Australian Baha'i
- First American Baha'i
- Contributing to the Fund
- Teaching

When we say we are Baha'i what does it mean?

In very simple terms a Baha'i is a follower of Baha'u'llah. That means Baha'is believe Baha'u'llah is the Messenger of God for today and wholeheartedly practice his teachings and principles and obey his laws. Keep in mind that all Baha'is are striving to become a true Baha'i — the Baha'i standard is very high. The only 'true' Baha'i was Abdu'l-Baha, which is why one of his titles is 'The Exemplar'. He lived His life as an example for all Baha'is. Below are a couple of quotes by Abdu'l-Baha regarding the qualities of a Baha'i.

> "If he is a Baha'i in reality, his deeds and actions will be decisive proofs of it. What are the requirements? Love for mankind, sincerity toward all, reflecting the oneness of the world of humanity, **philanthropy**, becoming enkindled with the fire of the love of God, attainment to the knowledge of God and that which is conducive to human welfare." (Abdu'l-Baha, *The Promulgation of Universal Peace*, p. 336)

> "In brief, let each one of you be as a lamp shining forth with the light of the virtues of the world of humanity. Be trustworthy, sincere, affectionate and replete with chastity. Be illumined, be spiritual, be divine, be glorious, be quickened of God, be a Baha'i." (Abdu'l-Baha, *The Promulgation of Universal Peace*, p. 453)

How can we practice our virtues? What is the best way to practice your virtues?

Throughout the writings there are many references regarding the importance of acquiring virtues. There are so many virtues – where do you begin? Abdu'l-Baha said, "Truthfulness is the foundation of all virtues of the world of humanity. Without truthfulness progress and success in all the worlds of God are impossible for a soul. When this holy attribute is established in man, all the divine qualities will also become realised." (*Baha'i World Faith*, p. 384)

How successful you are in developing virtues that you find difficult to practice depends on how hard you really try. Baha'u'llah said, "Success or failure, gain or loss, must, therefore, depend upon man's own exertions. The more he striveth, the greater will be his progress." (*Gleanings*, pp. 81–2)

How do we acquire virtues? Abdu'l-Baha listed several things we need to have in order to help us acquire virtues.

> "... First, through the knowledge of God. Second, through the love of God. Third, through faith. Fourth, through philanthropic deeds. Fifth, through self-sacrifice. Sixth, through severance from this world. Seventh, through sanctity and holiness." (Abdu'l-Baha, *The Promulgation of Universal Peace*, p. 226)

There is also the power of prayer. You can pray to Baha'u'llah to help you to develop and practice the virtues. "You must supplicate and pray to God every night and every day, seeking His assistance and help ..." (Abdu'l-Baha, *The Promulgation of Universal Peace*, p. 458)

Why don't we have more Baha'is around the World?

At present the Baha'i community is very much a minority and there are many people around the world who have not even heard of the Baha'i Faith as yet. The Universal House of Justice makes the following comments on this situation:

> "Mankind's response to the Message of Baha'u'llah has been dangerously, one might say disastrously, slow. From the earliest days it has been brought to the notice of the leaders and scholars, but few of these, very few, have rallied to its support. The most profound and most widespread response has been from the middle classes and indeed from the poor, the unlettered, the deprived and the suffering." (*Universal House of Justice*, 1963–1986: 195.2)

> "The Universal House of Justice is aware of the magnitude of the problems that the Baha'i communities face, but as the response to the Message of Baha'u'llah increases and as the Baha'i community throughout the world shows its ability to overcome these problems, the attention of men and women of every stratum of society will increasingly be drawn to the Faith. The most urgent need now — so late is the hour — is for the Baha'is to spread the Message, while they are still able to do so, to the largest possible number of their fellow human beings, simultaneously expanding and consolidating the Baha'i community as quickly as they can with the resources at their disposal. As mankind passes through the darkest phase of its history, the Baha'i community will have to face not only entry by troops, which it is now experiencing, but, before too long, mass conversion." (*Universal House of Justice*, 1963–1986: 195.4)

If all of the Baha'is had followed Abdu'l-Baha's advice to each teach one person a year, the Baha'i Faith would be doubling every year!

Who was the first Baha'i in Australia?

Clara and John Hyde Dunn pioneered to Australia on the 10th April 1920. Clara and John were both born in London. They first met one another around 1906–1907 when John was already a Baha'i. During a train ride John struck up a conversation with Clara and spoke to her about the Baha'i Faith and invited her to a public meeting that night on the Baha'i Faith. As a result, Clara later became a Baha'i.

Both John and Clara had married other people and ended up immigrating to the United States of America. Years later, when they were both widowed and residing in San Francisco, they reacquainted and later married.

It was in 1920 that they decided to pioneer to Australia. In Australia John Dunn obtained a job with a Melbourne firm which enabled him to travel with Clara all over Australia and New Zealand and therefore teach the Faith.

The first real believer in Australia to declare was Oswald Whitaker, an optometrist, who lived in Sydney. He was a member of the National Spiritual Assembly of the Baha'is of Australia and New Zealand from its formation in 1934 until his passing in July 1942.

Clara and John often referred to each other as 'Mother' and 'Father' and as a result were referred to as 'Mother' and 'Father' Dunn by the Australian Baha'i community and throughout the world.

In February 1941, John Hyde Dunn passed away to the Abha Kingdom. He was later elevated to the station of Hand of the Cause of God. In February 1952 Clara Dunn was also elevated to the station of Hand of the Cause of God. Clara passed away in November 1960. Both of their bodies were laid to rest in Sydney at the Woronora Cemetery.

Who was the first Baha'i in America?

The first American Baha'i was Thornton Chase. Thornton Chase was born in Springfield, in Massachusetts on 22 February 1847. He initially joined the United States Military during the American Civil War, rising to the rank of Captain. After the war he went to Brown University. After graduating from University, he moved to Chicago and became an insurance salesman.

Thornton always had an interest in religion. He attended a meeting in 1894 on the Baha'i Faith. The guest speaker was Dr Ibrahim Khayru'llah, a Syrian from Egypt. During that year Thornton became a Baha'i.

Fortunately, Thornton's position as an insurance salesman enabled him to travel frequently and therefore provided him with the opportunity to tell many people about the teachings of the Baha'i Faith.

In 1907, Thornton went on Pilgrimage to Akka and met with Abdu'l-Baha on several occasions. He documented his pilgrimage experience in a book entitled 'In Galilee'. Later Thornton wrote another book that was published in 1919, several years after his death. It was entitled 'The Baha'i Revelation'.

Thornton Chase ascended to the next world on 30 September 1912 following an illness that lasted for several weeks. His body was laid to rest In Los Angeles, California. Abdu'l-Baha was in San Francisco when he heard of Thornton's passing. Abdu'l-Baha travelled to Los Angeles to pay his last respects to Thornton by praying at the gravesite.

Who can contribute to the Baha'i Fund?

Only Baha'is can contribute to the Baha'i Fund. "One of the distinguishing features of the Cause of God is its principle of non-acceptance of financial contributions for its own purposes from non-Baha'is: support of the Baha'i Fund is a bounty reserved by Baha'u'llah to His declared followers. This bounty imposes full responsibility for financial support of the Faith on the believers alone." (Letter from the Universal House of Justice to the Baha'is of the World, Naw-Ruz 1974)

> "Giving to the Fund, therefore, is a spiritual privilege not open to those who have not accepted Baha'u'llah, of which no believer should deny himself. It is both a responsibility and a source of bounty." (Letter from Universal House of Justice to all National Spiritual Assemblies, 7 August 1985)

If, however, a person who is not a Baha'i wishes to make a donation to the Baha'i Fund then it is permissible to accept the gift, making it clear that the money will be used solely for charitable or humanitarian purposes. This is explained in the following quote by Shoghi Effendi:

> "In cases ... when a friend or sympathiser of the Faith eagerly insists on a monetary contribution for the promotion of the Faith, such gifts should be accepted and duly acknowledged by the elected representatives of the believers with the express understanding that they would be utilised by them only to reinforce that section of the Baha'i Fund exclusively devoted to **philanthropic** or charitable purposes." (Letter to the Baha'is of the United States and Canada, dated 25 October 1929)

How much is enough to pay to the Baha'i fund? As a child can I contribute even a few dollars?

An important aspect of giving to the Baha'i Fund is the spirit of **sacrifice**. Even the poorest of Baha'is are required to donate to the Baha'i Fund. Shoghi Effendi said, "… There can be no limit to one's contribution to the national fund. The more one can give the better it is, especially when such offerings necessitate the sacrifice of other wants and desires on the part of the donor. The harder the sacrifice the more meritorious will it be, of course, in the sight of God. For after all it is not so much the quantity of one's offerings that matters, but rather the measure of deprivation that such offerings entail …" (Letter to an individual believer, 31 December 1935, *Lights of Guidance*, p. 250)

Baha'i children can of course give money to the Baha'i Fund. Every dollar helps and is needed. "… God does not ask from any soul except according to his ability. This contribution must come from all cities and villages from all the believers of God … Whosoever comes with one good act, God will give him tenfold. There is no doubt that the living Lord shall assist and confirm the generous soul." (Abdu'l-Baha, *Lights of Guidance*, p. 250)

A few dollars donated by a child is often a very generous act requiring sacrifice. That money could have been easily spent by that child on junk food, magazines or the latest gadgets.

How do you know when someone is ready to hear about the Baha'i Faith?

Teaching your friends requires a number of virtues. Virtues like courage, patience, tact, humility and wisdom are needed. Courage is required because sometimes it is not easy being different and it is often our own fear of rejection by our friends that holds us back.

The first step in teaching is becoming friends. Gradually over time as your friends show interest, teach them different aspects of the Baha'i Faith. Start off telling them about areas of the Faith that may be of interest to them. For example, maybe a friend or relative has recently died and you could share the Baha'i point of view on the next world. You may have a friend concerned about poverty in developing countries, or the conflicts and wars in the world — this would be a good opportunity to share the some of the principles of the Baha'i Faith.

Tell your friends why you are a Baha'i and the things you love about being a Baha'i. Not everyone will respond enthusiastically or appear to show an interest in the Baha'i Faith, so this is where patience comes in handy. The following quotes highlight the importance of the above virtues and some useful tips to keep in mind while teaching.

Abdu'l-Baha wrote, "The friends of God should weave bonds of fellowship with others and show absolute love and affection towards them. These links have deep influence on people, and they will listen. When the friends sense receptivity to the Word of God, they should deliver the Message with wisdom." (cited in *The Path Toward Spirituality*, p. 39)

> "They must first try and remove any apprehensions in the people they teach. In fact, every one of the believers should choose one person every year and try to establish ties of friendship with him, so that all his fear would disappear. Only

then, and gradually, must he teach that person. This is the best method. (Abdu'l-Baha, 'The Individual and Teaching' cited in *Unrestrained as the Wind*, 1985, p. 89)

Baha'u'lllah further writes, "Help him to see and recognise the truth, without esteeming yourself to be, in the least, superior to him, or to be possessed of greater endowments." (*Gleanings from the Writings of Baha'u'llah*, p. 8)

"Teaching the Cause of God is not only through the tongue; it is through deeds, a good disposition, happiness of nature, kindness and sympathy, good fellowship, trustworthiness, holiness, virtue, purity of ideals, and lastly, speech." (Abdu'l-Baha: *Lights of Guidance*, p. 591)

"As the Guardian himself has pointed out **audacity** in teaching is essential, but no less important is the necessity for the exercise of the utmost tact, wisdom and consideration, in approaching either separate individuals or large public audiences. Only when these qualities have been duly combined and harmonised can the teaching work be carried on effectively and produce lasting results." (*Lights of Guidance*, p. 601)

Glossary

Acquiesce: to consent to someone's wishes without protest.
Annihilated: completely destroyed.
Audacity: bold and without fear.
Authenticity: real and genuine.
Avarice: greediness for wealth.
Celestial: divine and heavenly.
Corporeal: physical or having to do with the body; not spiritual.
Countenance: face or expression of a face.
Culmination: the highest point.
Déjà vu: a feeling of having experienced something before it has occurred.
Edifice: a large building.
Effacement: to erase.
Entity: existence or being.
Galvanise: to cause to move; to excite and stimulate.
Inevitable: will happen for certain.
Metaphor: a figure of speech in which something is spoken of as if it were something else.
Phenomena: people or things that are beyond ordinary; remarkable and extraordinary.
Philanthropy: the practice of performing charitable acts or wanting to help other people.
Sacrifice: to give up something of value.
Sanctified: holy and associated with God.

Bibliography

Abdu'l-Baha, *Paris Talks*, Baha'i Publishing Trust, London, 1972.
Abdu'l-Baha, *Selections from the Writings of Abdu'l-Baha*, Baha'i World Centre, Haifa, 1978.
Abdu'l-Baha, *Some Answered Questions*, Baha'i Publishing Trust, Wilmette, 1991.
Abdu'l-Baha, *The Promulgation of Universal Peace*, Baha'i Publishing Trust, Wilmette, 1982.
Abdu'l-Baha, *Writings and Utterances of Abdu'l-Baha*, Baha'i Publishing Trust, New Dehli, 2000.
Alexander, M., *Christianity Renewed. Vol. 2*, Baha'i Publishing Trust, India,1998.
Baha'i Education: A Compilation, Baha'i Publishing Trust, Wilmette, 1977.
Baha'u'llah, *Epistle to the Son of the Wolf*, Baha'i Publishing Trust, Wilmette, 1962.
Baha'u'llah, *Gleanings from the Writings of Baha'u'llah*, Baha'i Publishing Trust, Wilmette,1983.
Baha'u'llah, *The Hidden Words and Selected Holy Writings*. Baha'i Publishing Trust Committee, Malaysia.
Baha'u'llah, *The Kitab-i-Aqdas: The Most Holy Book,* Baha'i Publications, Australia, 1993.
Baha'u'llah, *The Kitab-i-Iqan: The Book of Certitude*, Baha'i Publishing Trust, Wilmette, 1974.
Baha'u'llah, *Writings of Baha'u'llah*, Baha'i Publishing Trust, New Dehli, 1986.
Hornby, H., *Lights of Guidance: A Baha'i Reference File*, Baha'i Publishing Trust, India, 1994.
Khan, J. and Khan, P., *Advancement of Women: A Baha'i Perspective*, Baha'i Publishing Trust, Wilmette, 1998.
Life Death and Immortality: The Journey of the Soul, Baha'i Publishing Trust, Wilmette, 1994.
Messages from the Universal House of Justice: 1963–1986, The Third Epoch of the Formative Age', Baha'i Publishing Trust, Wilmette,1996
Paine, M., *The Divine Art of Living*, Baha'i Publishing Trust, Wilmette, 1986.

Shoghi Effendi, *God Passes By*, Baha'i Publishing Trust, Wilmette, 1965.
Shoghi Effendi, *The Promised Day is Come*, Baha'i Publishing Trust, Wilmette, 1961.
Unrestrained as the Wind: A Life Dedicated to Baha'u'llah, Baha'i Publishing Trust, Wilmette, 1985.
Unto Him Shall We Return, Baha'i Publishing Trust, Wilmette, 1985.
Vafai, S., *The Path Toward Spirituality*, Palabra Publications, Florida, 1996.
Waging Peace, Kalimat Press, Los Angeles, 1984.
<http://bahailibrary.com?file=hassall_bahai_community_randwick.html>
<http://news.bbc.co.uk/2/low/health/background_briefings/smoking/281167.stm?
<http://www.bci.org/reno/chase.htm>
<http://www.nsw.bahai.org.au/hawkesbury/mfd.htm>

www.ingramcontent.com/pod-product-compliance
Lightning Source LLC
Chambersburg PA
CBHW072100290426
44110CB00014B/1757